223.2
An 4   Angel, Marie, illus.
            The Twentythird psalm.

DATE | ISSUED TO

223.2
An 4   Angel, Marie, illus.
            The Twentythird psalm.

Temple Israel Library
Minneapolis, Minn.

Please sign your full name on the above card.

Return books promptly to the Library or Temple Office.

Fines will be charged for overdue books or for damage or loss of same.

THE TWENTYTHIRD PSALM

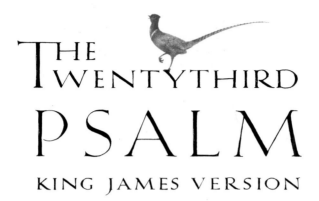

THE TWENTYTHIRD PSALM

KING JAMES VERSION

ILLUSTRATED BY
MARIE ANGEL

THOMAS Y. CROWELL COMPANY
NEW YORK

1   2   3   4   5   6   7   8   9   10

Printed in Great Britain by Lund Humphries

THE
TWENTYTHIRD
PSALM

THE
LORD
IS MY
SHEPHERD ;

I

SHALL
NOT
WANT.

HE
MAKETH ME
TO LIE DOWN
IN GREEN
PASTURES:

HE LEADETH
ME BESIDE THE
STILL WATERS.

HE
RESTORETH
MY SOUL:

HE

LEADETH ME IN THE PATHS OF RIGHTEOUSNESS

FOR
HIS NAME'S
SAKE.

YEA
THOUGH
I WALK

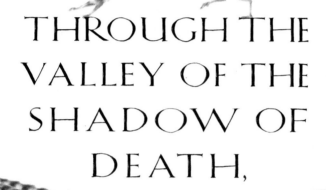

THROUGH THE
VALLEY OF THE
SHADOW OF
DEATH,

I WILL FEAR
NO EVIL : FOR
THOU ART
WITH ME;

THY ROD AND THY STAFF THEY COMFORT ME.

THOU

PREPAREST A
TABLE BEFORE ME

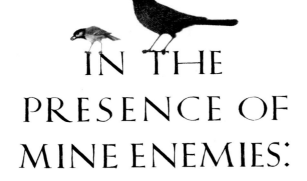

IN THE
PRESENCE OF
MINE ENEMIES:

THOU ANOINTEST MY HEAD WITH OIL;

MY CUP
RUNNETH
OVER.

SURELY

GOODNESS AND MERCY SHALL FOLLOW ME

ALL THE DAYS
OF MY LIFE:

AND I WILL
DWELL IN THE
HOUSE OF THE
LORD

FOR EVER.

19

ABOUT THE ARTIST

Marie Angel's fondness for all small creatures is beautifully expressed in her miniature paintings. Miss Angel's work has been widely exhibited in her native England as well as in this country at several museums, including the Hunt Botanical Library in Pittsburgh.

Miss Angel devotes most of her working hours to calligraphy and miniature painting. She did the exquisite drawings that are reproduced in *Two Bestiaries*, published by the Department of Printing and Graphics of the Harvard College Library. These tiny books, with their sensitive and meticulous drawings, have earned Miss Angel a wide and appreciative audience. In 1968 she illustrated *We Went Looking*, a poem especially written for her by poet Aileen Fisher.

Born in London, Marie Angel studied there in the School of Design of the Royal College of Art and received her diploma while specializing in calligraphy. Miss Angel lives in Surrey, England.